SOME MAJOR EVENTS IN WORLD WAR II

THE EUROPEAN THEATER

1939 SEPTEMBER—Germany invades Poland Great Britain, France, Australia, & New Zealand declare war on Germany; Battle of the Atlantic begins. NOVEMBER—Russia invades Finland.

1940 APRIL—Germany invades Denmark & Norway. MAY—Germany invades Belgium, Luxembourg, & The Netherlands; British forces retreat to Dunkirk and escape to England. JUNE—Italy declares war on Britain & France; France surrenders to Germany. JULY—Battle of Britain begins. SEPTEMBER—Italy invades Egypt; Germany, Italy, & Japan form the Axis countries. OCTOBER—Italy invades Greece. NOVEMBER—Battle of Britain over. DECEMBER—Britain attacks Italy in North Africa.

1941 JANUARY—Allies take Tobruk. FEBRUARY—Rommel arrives at Tripoli. APRIL—Germany invades Greece & Yugoslavia. JUNE—Allies are in Syria; Germany invades Russia. JULY—Russia joins Allies. AUGUST—Germans capture Kiev. OCTOBER—Germany reaches Moscow. DECEMBER—Germans retreat from Moscow; Japan attacks Pearl Harbor; United States enters war against Axis nations.

1942 MAY—first British bomber attack on Cologne. JUNE—Germans take Tobruk. SEPTEMBER—Battle of Stalingrad begins. OCTOBER—Battle of El Alamein begins. NOVEMBER—Allies recapture Tobruk; Russians counterattack at Stalingrad.

1943 JANUARY—Allies take Tripoli. FEBRUARY—German troops at Stalingrad surrender. APRIL—revolt of Warsaw Ghetto Jews begins. MAY—German and Italian resistance in North Africa is over; their troops surrender in Tunisia; Warsaw Ghetto revolt is put down by Germany. JULY—allies invade Sicily; Mussolini put in prison. SEPTEMBER—Allies land in Italy; Italians surrender; Germans occupy Rome; Mussolini rescued by Germany. OCTOBER—Allies capture Naples; Italy declares war on Germany. NOVEMBER—Russians recapture Kiev.

1944 JANUARY—Allies land at Anzio. JUNE—Rome falls to Allies; Allies land in Normandy (D-Day). JULY—assassination attempt on Hitler fails. AUGUST—Allies land in southern France. SEPTEMBER—Brussels freed. OCTOBER—Athens liberated. DECEMBER—Battle of the Bulge.

1945 JANUARY—Russians free Warsaw. FEBRUARY—Dresden bombed. APRIL—Americans take Belsen and Buchenwald concentration camps; Russians free Vienna; Russians take over Berlin; Mussolini killed; Hitler commits suicide. MAY—Germany surrenders; Goering captured.

THE PACIFIC THEATER

1940 SEPTEMBER—Japan joins Axis nations Germany & Italy.

1941 APRIL—Russia & Japan sign neutrality pact. DECEMBER—Japanese launch attacks against Pearl Harbor, Hong Kong, the Philippines, & Malaya; United States and Allied nations declare war on Japan; China declares war on Japan, Germany, & Italy; Japan takes over Guam, Wake Island, & Hong Kong; Japan attacks Burma.

1942 JANUARY—Japan takes over Manila; Japan invades Dutch East Indies. FEBRUARY—Japan takes over Singapore; Battle of the Java Sea. APRIL—Japanese overrun Bataan. MAY—Japan takes Mandalay; Allied forces in Philippines surrender to Japan; Japan takes Corregidor; Battle of the Coral Sea. JUNE—Battle of Midway; Japan occupies Aleutian Islands. AUGUST—United States invades Guadalcanal in the Solomon Islands.

1943 FEBRUARY—Guadalcanal taken by U.S. Marines. MARCH—Japanese begin to retreat in China. APRIL—Yamamoto shot down by U.S. Air Force. MAY—U.S. troops take Aleutian Islands back from Japan. JUNE—Allied troops land in New Guinea. NOVEMBER—U.S. Marines invade Bougainville & Tarawa.

1944 FEBRUARY—Truk liberated. JUNE—Saipan attacked by United States. JULY—battle for Guam begins. OCTOBER—U.S. troops invade Philippines; Battle of Leyte Gulf won by Allies.

1945 JANUARY—Luzon taken; Burma Road won back. MARCH—Iwo Jima freed. APRIL—Okinawa attacked by U.S. troops; President Franklin Roosevelt dies; Harry S. Truman becomes president. JUNE—United States takes Okinawa. AUGUST—atomic bomb dropped on Hiroshima; Russia declares war on Japan; atomic bomb dropped on Nagasaki. SEPTEMBER—Japan surrenders.

WORLD AT WAR

The Holocaust

WORLD AT WAR

The Holocaust

By R. Conrad Stein

Consultant:
Professor Robert L. Messer, Ph.D.
Department of History
University of Illinois, Chicago

CHILDRENS PRESS®
CHICAGO

When American soldiers entered the Nazi concentration camps near
the end of World War II, they came upon sights that horrified them.
Those entering Belsen found this open grave filled with bodies.

FRONTISPIECE:
Adolf Hitler, the Nazi *Fuehrer* (leader) who planned
the extermination of all the Jews of Europe

**Library of Congress Cataloging in
Publication Data**

Stein, R. Conrad.
  The Holocaust.

  (World at war)
  Includes index.
  Summary: A revelation of the atrocities
committed against European Jews by Hitler and the
Nazis during World War II.
  1. Holocaust, Jewish (1939-1945)—Juvenile
literature. [1. Holocaust, Jewish (1939-1945)]
I. Title. II. Series.
D810.J4S754 1986 940.53'15'03924 85-31415
ISBN 0-516-04767-1

PICTURE CREDITS:
NATIONAL ARCHIVES: Cover, pages 6, 9, 16, 22, 23
(top), 24 (bottom), 27, 30 (left), 32 (top left), 39, 42
(top), 43 (center right)
LIBRARY OF CONGRESS: Pages 4, 19
WIDE WORLD: Pages 10, 12 (bottom), 15, 18
(bottom), 21, 23 (bottom), 28, 31, 32 (top right),
33, 37 (right), 40, 43 (top right, center left, bottom
left and right), 44
HISTORICAL PICTURES SERVICE, INC., CHICAGO: Pages
11, 12 (center), 13, 14, 29 (top), 34
UPI: Pages 12 (top), 17, 32 (center), 35, 43 (top left),
46
HILLSTROM STOCK PHOTOS: © ART BROWN
COLLECTION: Pages 18 (top), 24 (top left and right),
26, 30 (right)
PHOTRI: Pages 29 (bottom), 32 (bottom), 42
(bottom)
THE BETTMANN ARCHIVES: Page 37 (left)

COVER PHOTO:
These survivors of the Holocaust were among those
found when the Allies liberated the Nazi
concentration camps at the end of World War II.

PROJECT EDITOR:
Joan Downing

CREATIVE DIRECTOR:
Margrit Fiddle

In the spring of 1945, a company of American soldiers sweeping through Germany entered a barbed-wire-enclosed camp. An officer named Curtis Mitchell came upon a sight that turned him to ice. In a trenchlike grave, he saw a pile of naked bodies stacked up like firewood. "[The dead] were so thin and dried out that they might have been monkeys or plaster of paris and you had to keep saying to yourself, these were human beings, and when you said it your mind was not believing it because nothing like this had ever happened before and it just couldn't happen."

But as the whole world soon discovered, it did happen. The end of the war revealed the grim fact that Germany's Nazis had committed mass murder against Europe's Jews. This dark period in human history is known as the Holocaust.

Long before the onset of World War II, Germany's Nazi party leader, Adolf Hitler, had decreed it his mission to eradicate the Jewish people from Europe. Other groups, including Gypsies and the disabled, also became targets for the Nazis. However, during World War II, the German leaders concentrated their efforts on the systematic elimination of Jews. At the start of the war, about eleven million Jews lived in Europe. By 1945, six million or so had died at the hands of the Nazis. Never before had organized murder taken place in such appalling magnitude.

The reasons for this tragedy will never be fully understood. But a study of the Holocaust must start with the long history of hatred, mistrust, and persecution that the Jews of Europe have suffered.

Jews have lived in this Rumanian ghetto for centuries.

In ancient times the Jewish homeland, Israel, fell to a series of conquerors, and the Jews scattered to various parts of the world. In every European state where they settled, Jews were a minority. Because they practiced a different religion, they suffered persecution. In the Middle Ages, European Jews were required to live in walled-off sections of cities called ghettos. They were forbidden to own land and were not allowed to join craft unions. Consequently, many became merchants and money changers; those occupations alone amplified the hostilities Europeans felt toward the Jewish minorities.

After World War I, widespread unemployment forced many Germans to seek food from municipal kitchens. Bread lines like this one were common.

In the eighteenth and nineteenth centuries, a pattern of anti-Jewish sentiment (anti-Semitism) developed in Europe. In times of peace and prosperity, Europeans accepted the presence of Jews in their midst. When war or economic problems plagued their lands, however, the Europeans blamed those woes on the Jewish people. European leaders, especially, were quick to claim that Jewish influence was behind whatever misfortune struck their nations.

Until the Nazi era, German anti-Semitism was no more vicious than that of other European nations. The aftermath of World War I left Germany in economic chaos, however, and into the turmoil stepped the fledgling Nazi party and the fiery Adolf Hitler.

Nazi stormtroopers go into action during Adolf Hitler's 1923 revolt *(Putsch)* against the German government.

Among those who participated in the ill-fated *Putsch* were (from left) Dr. Friedrich Weber, Wilhelm Frick, Colonel Hermann Kriebel, General Erich von Ludendorff, Hitler, Lieutenent Wilhelm Brückner, Captain Ernst Röhm, and Adolf Wagner.

The Nazi leader's road to power began after the failure of his 1923 revolt against the German government. Hitler was arrested, convicted, and forced to serve a nine-month jail term. While in prison, he wrote *Mein Kampf (My Struggle),* in which he blamed the Jews for all the ills of Germany and the world: "Was there any shady undertaking, any form of foulness . . . in which at least one Jew did not participate?"

Shortly after his release
from prison in 1924,
Hitler visited a Bavarian
Nazi party group (above).
He saluted his growing
band of followers during
a 1927 party parade in
Nuremberg (right).
Julius Streicher, the most
fanatical anti-Semite in
the Nazi party, stirred up
this huge crowd in Berlin
in 1935 (below). Banners
in the hall carry such
slogans as "The Jews Are
Our Ruin" and "The Jews
Are Our Disaster."

Nazi propaganda minister Joseph Goebbels (above) ranted against the Jews long before Hitler came to power in 1933.

In the tradition of European anti-Semitism, Hitler and the Nazis claimed that Jewish bankers had caused the economic collapse, that Jewish political intrigue had engineered Germany's defeat in World War I, and that Jewish-backed Communist elements were poised to take over the nation. "The Jews are to blame for everything," said Nazi propaganda minister Joseph Goebbels.

"Die, Jew" is the curse that defaced this Jewish synagogue
in Düsseldorf in 1933 after Hitler came to power in Germany.

After becoming chancellor of Germany in 1933,
Hitler launched a reign of terror against the
nation's Jews. Nazi thugs called Brownshirts beat
up Jews on the streets while police officers stood
by pretending not to notice. Swaggering
Brownshirts roamed German cities singing the
new party song, the "Horst Wessel Lied," one
verse of which was: "When Jewish blood spurts
from the knife/Then all will be fine." The windows
of Jewish-owned shops were broken and epithets
such as "Jew Pig" were scribbled on the walls.

The windows of this Jewish shop were among the hundreds that were broken in towns all over Germany during *Kristallnacht*.

The German Jews' darkest hour of the prewar years came in November, 1938. In Paris, an enraged Jewish teenager, whose family recently had been deported from Germany, shot and killed a minor German diplomat. At home, the Nazis took revenge by unleashing a bloodbath. In one terrible night, the dreaded Brownshirts killed a hundred Jews, and assaulted many more. At least twenty thousand Jewish people were arrested on trumped-up charges. Synagogues all over Germany were set to the torch. The bloody November evening came to be known as *Kristallnacht* (Crystal Night) because the streets of German cities were littered with shards of glass from hundreds of broken store windows.

Even very young children were taught Nazi propaganda, including anti-Semitism.

The Jews arrested during *Kristallnacht* were herded into compounds called concentration camps. Most were released after a brief stay, but their imprisonment for no crime other than being Jewish was a harbinger of the awful days to come. The grim future could also be foreseen in this speech Hitler delivered shortly before the outbreak of World War II: "During my struggle for power, the Jews laughed at my prophecies that I would some day assume leadership of the state. I suppose that the laughter of Jewry is now choking in their throats. Today I will be a prophet again. If

Early in the Nazi reign of terror against the Jews, Jews all over Germany were constantly humiliated. These Jews of Chemnitz, Saxony were rounded up by Nazi troops and forced to whitewash walls and clean the streets of the town. At this time, very few people believed that the Nazis were actually planning to exterminate the Jews.

internationally financed Jewry should succeed once more in plunging the people into another world war, then the consequence will not be a victory of Jewry, but on the contrary, the destruction of the Jewish race in Europe."

Both the German and the Jewish communities interpreted "the destruction of the Jewish race" to mean the further humiliation of Jews and denial of more of their rights. Very few outside of party circles could imagine that the Nazis planned the mass slaughter of European Jews. Such a possibility was too fantastic even to consider.

Above: German troops on the way to invade Poland in 1939. The graffiti on the train says: "We're going to Poland to beat the hide off the Jews."
Below: Shortly after his successful lightning invasion of Poland, Hitler (at right, in leather coat) salutes a parade of tanks rolling down a Warsaw street.

Poles in Warsaw watched in horror as the German army paraded down the streets.

Hitler electrified the world on September 1, 1939, when he sent his tanks and infantry smashing into Poland, thereby launching World War II. Initially, the splendid German armies enjoyed sensational victories, and the Nazis believed themselves to be the masters of Europe. The start of the war also dropped a cloak of secrecy over Germany and its captured territories. Under cover of this wartime secrecy, the new masters of Europe began the systematic destruction of the Jewish people.

Immediately after conquering Poland, the German occupation force revived the medieval practice of forcing all Jews to live in walled-off ghettos. The great ghetto at Warsaw held nearly half a million people. Since the Nazis controlled the supplies that went into the ghetto, they at first tried to starve the ghetto dwellers. But there were even crueler plans for the Polish ghettos. As German officer Friedrich Uebekhoer said, "The creation of the ghetto is, of course, only a transitory measure. I shall determine at what time and with what means the ghetto . . . will be cleansed of Jews."

In captured Russian territory, the Nazis took a more direct approach to eliminate the Jewish population. Jews were herded onto remote farms, stripped of their clothing, and machine-gunned to death. The Nazi leaders quickly discovered that regular army troops were unsuitable for carrying out such mass murder. German soldiers, even though they were known to be obedient, refused to

Steel-helmeted, black-coated SS troops carried out Hitler's dirty work.

gun down naked civilians. So the job was turned over to the *Schutzstaffel* (SS). This "protective guard" originally was Hitler's handpicked bodyguard regiment. During the war, the ranks of the SS expanded. They were special troops, all dedicated Nazis, who believed that Adolf Hitler was next to God. Many SS men had been members of the brutal Brownshirt organization. SS *Einsatzgruppen* (special action groups) were volunteers who carried out the dirtiest of Hitler's dirty work. Some reports indicate that these SS assassination units found pleasure in machine-gunning defenseless Jews.

There is no painless way to tell the details of the Holocaust story. The words of Rivka Yosselevscka, a young Russian Jewish woman who was captured by an SS killing squad in August of 1942, tell part of the story: "We saw people naked, lined up. But we were still hoping that this was only torture. Maybe there is hope — hope of the living. . . . When it came to our turn, our father was beaten. We prayed, we begged. . . . Then they tore the clothing off the old man and he was shot. I saw it with my own eyes. And they took my mother and shot her too; and then there was my grandmother. . . ." Finally, the young woman herself was shot in the head by an SS guard. Miraculously, she survived to tell her tale to a court after the war.

Mass executions of Soviet civilians—Jews and others—were a common occurrence during the German invasion of Russia. On the opposite page, residents of Kerch search for relatives among the bodies left by the Germans.
Left: In this captured German photograph, the Russians about to be executed stand on the edge of a trench into which those previously executed have fallen.
Below: The Germans hanged these Russian civilians and set fire to their village.

Many of the death-camp victims were rounded up from the ghettos of eastern Europe (above right and below). They were packed into boxcars (above left) for the long and agonizing journey to the camps.

As the war years dragged on, the slaying of Jews became even more merciless—and more efficient. In occupied Poland, as well as Germany and even Holland, the now-infamous camps were built. Some were designed to kill people on a gruesome, assembly-line basis.

Most of the death-camp victims came from the ghettos of eastern Europe. Many of the starving ghetto dwellers were lured out of their confines by promises of work and regular meals. Their agony began with a long and terrifying train ride. Men, women, and children were packed into boxcars, sixty to a hundred people per car. With little food or water and no toilet facilities for the passengers, the trains wound over carefully selected routes designed to avoid cities. Few civilians would ever hear the moans of those trapped inside the cars. The trip to a camp could take as long as ten days. One survivor of such a train ride recalled, "The children cried, the sick groaned, the old people lamented. . . . We lost all concept of human behavior."

Those boxcar passengers who were still alive when they arrived at the camps were divided into two groups (above). One group would be sent to the gas chambers. The other, composed of the healthiest of the victims, would be used for slave labor.

At the gateway to the camps, a Nazi doctor or an SS officer determined which Jews should live to perform slave labor, and which should die. Typically, the officer or doctor looked over the new arrivals and motioned the healthy-looking men to the right and most of the women, the children, and the sickly to the left. Those sent to the left were doomed.

American troops who overran the Dachau death camp inspect the "shower room" (left) and the door (right) to one of the gas chambers.

In larger camps such as Auschwitz and Treblinka, the captives destined to die were taken to specially designed gas chambers. To prevent panic, the guards often told the Jews they were going to take showers. In many camps, the people were instructed to take off their clothes and hang them on numbered pegs. They were advised to remember their number so the clothes could be reclaimed "after the bath." One camp even issued towels to the captives. If any group suspected trickery and began to riot, the guards whipped or clubbed them into line.

Rudolf Hoess, commander of Auschwitz (not to be confused with Adolf Hitler aide Rudolf Franz Hess), told a war crimes court that two and a half million people were executed there and that another half million died of starvation.

The names of the large camps that specialized in death by gassing will always remain as indelible scars in the grisly Holocaust story—Auschwitz, Belzec, Chelmno, Majdanek, Sobibor, Treblinka. The camp at Auschwitz, in particular, has long symbolized the despair of the era. At that fortress ringed by barbed wire, four huge gas chambers could produce six thousand corpses a day. The commander of Auschwitz, ex-convict Rudolf Hoess, later told a court that two and a half million people were executed there, and that another half million died of starvation.

Left: The barbed wire, moat, and guard tower at Dachau.
Below: When the Americans seized the Buchenwald death camp, this body of a prisoner was found dangling from a hook in the yard. German civilians from nearby Weimar were brought to the camp and forced to view the evidence of Nazi atrocities.

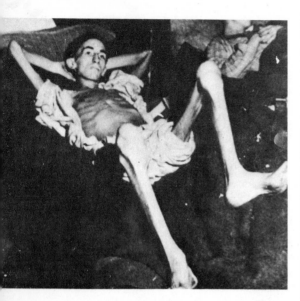

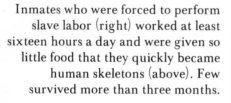

Inmates who were forced to perform slave labor (right) worked at least sixteen hours a day and were given so little food that they quickly became human skeletons (above). Few survived more than three months.

Those chosen to perform slave labor were forced to work sixteen or more hours a day. They were given little food and were subjected to harsh punishment if their work failed to please the guards. Few of the captive laborers survived more than three months, and very quickly the living began to envy the dead.

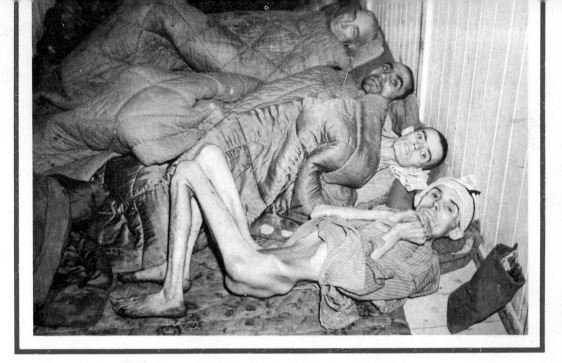

These emaciated Jews were inmates of Buchenwald concentration camp.

When American reporter Percy Knauth entered a recently liberated labor camp in early 1945, he found men who looked like skin stretched over skeletons. Knauth wrote, "If [the prisoners] moved at all, it was with a crawling slowness that made them look like huge, lethargic spiders. Many just lay in their bunks as if dead." Knauth reached into his pocket and offered one of the emaciated men a chocolate bar. "A dozen hands reached for the chocolate bar, clutching wildly. The filthy bodies pressed around me, pushed me, nearly knocked me down. . . . I saw the chocolate in several filthy hands, brown melted gobs of it—then it was gone."

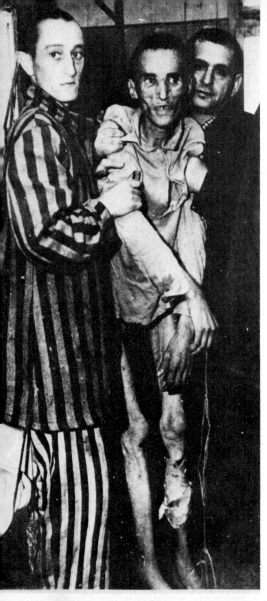

These victims of Nazi atrocities were found at Dachau (above), Webbelin (left), Belsen (below), and Buchenwald (bottom).

SS Colonel Adolf Eichmann was field coordinator of the Nazi concentration and extermination camps.

SS Colonel Adolf Eichmann served as field coordinator of the camps. His personality was a bizarre study in contrasts. Although he was a devoted Nazi, Eichmann was reluctant to view the inner workings of a gas chamber. "I simply cannot look at any suffering without trembling myself," he once said. Moreover, Eichmann was not a passionate anti-Semite as were his colleagues. He had a Jewish girlfriend, and even spoke a smattering of Yiddish. Eichmann was, instead, an obedient Nazi who accepted without question Hitler's preachings that Jewish culture was repugnant to the new German state.

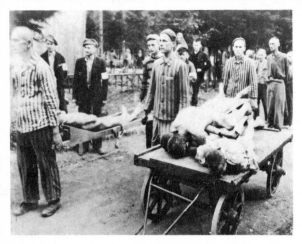

At Dachau, prisoners were forced to transport bodies to the ovens for burning (left). The bodies were then placed on stretchers (right) and shoved into the ovens.

From his high office, Eichmann engineered the machinery of death. He procured trains and boxcars to transport victims, even though railroad stock was vital to Germany's wartime economy. He also saw to it that furnaces for the burning of corpses were built at the camps. This letter dated February 12, 1943, which came from a German factory, may have crossed Eichmann's desk: "We acknowledge receipt of your order for five triple furnaces, including two electric elevators for the raising of corpses and one emergency elevator. A practical installation for stocking coal was also ordered, and one for transporting ashes." Eichmann did his job with typical German efficiency.

Grim-faced residents of Lublin peer into the ovens of Majdanek's crematory (above).
More furnaces were found at Buchenwald (below) and other Nazi extermination camps.

A particularly gruesome practice at the camps was the medical experimentation carried out by Nazi doctors. The doctors used camp inmates as human guinea pigs. Jews were not the only subjects singled out for these tests. Russian, Polish, and Gypsy prisoners of war were used as well.

Most of the medical experiments were designed to aid the military. For example, the German navy wanted to know how long sailors could live if they were stranded at sea. So several prisoners were given nothing but salt water to drink. To supply the air force with information on the ability of men to withstand high altitude, prisoners were locked into a specially built decompression chamber. An Austrian inmate named Anton Pacholegg later testified: "I have personally seen through the observation window of the decompression chamber when a prisoner inside would stand a vacuum until his lungs ruptured. . . . [The prisoners] would go mad and pull out their hair. . . . They would tear their heads and faces with their fingers and nails in an attempt to maim themselves in their madness."

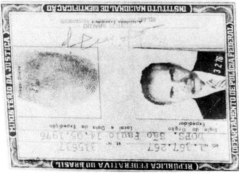

This Brazilian identity card in the name of Wolfgang Gerhard was once used by Josef Mengele (above), the "Angel of Death" who was the chief doctor at Auschwitz.

In other experiments, prisoners were plunged into vats of ice water to determine the body's resistance to cold. Some inmates were deliberately infected with deadly diseases such as typhus in order to test new drugs. All these ghastly experiments were conducted by doctors who had at one time in their careers pledged themselves to ease the suffering of others and to save lives.

The chief doctor at Auschwitz was a Nazi named Joseph Mengele. He came from a wealthy family and was said to be impeccably well mannered, cultured, and always neatly dressed. He sometimes whistled operatic arias while going about his work at the death camp.

Mengele greeted the new arrivals at Auschwitz, and with a flick of his wrist determined who would live and who would be gassed. Many of those who were spared the gas chamber became subjects in Mengele's special laboratory. The Nazi doctor performed bizarre tests on a variety of "subjects," including dwarfs and twins. The experiments, claimed this so-called Angel of Death, were for the purpose of finding ways to improve the racial stock of the German people. Mengele slipped out of Germany after the war. He fled to South America where he lived in hiding for nearly thirty-five years. It was confirmed in 1985 that Mengele drowned during a 1979 swimming accident in Brazil.

Though many of the Nazis' Jewish victims tried to fight back, they had few weapons and were weak after years of starvation. These Warsaw Ghetto rebels held out until the Germans had reduced the ghetto to rubble and ashes.

The awful activities at the camps reached their height during the war-torn years of 1943 and 1944—and the Jewish victims did their best to fight back. Inmates of the Treblinka death camp revolted. The Jews of the Warsaw ghetto staged a heroic battle. But the Jews had few weapons and were weak after years of deliberate starvation.

Though German Kurt Gerstein (left) risked his life to report the Nazis' massive extermination program against Europe's Jews, very few people believed his horror stories. Swedish diplomat Raoul Wallenberg (right) rescued more than twenty thousand Jews from extermination.

The people of German-occupied countries sometimes risked their lives to prevent the Nazis from taking Jews off to the camps. The Danes and the French were fearless in their efforts to protect their Jewish citizens. All too often, however, the well-armed and ruthless SS forces crushed all civilian resistance.

Finally, a handful of Germans who were aware of the systematic slaughter going on in the camps did their utmost to protect Jews. Kurt Gerstein was a German who joined the Nazi party as a youth, but quickly became disillusioned by the organization. As a party member, Gerstein was permitted to view the operation of a gas chamber. After the experience he wrote: "Men of the squad opened the wooden doors [of the chamber]. The dead were standing upright like basalt pillars, pressed together in the chamber. There would not have been room to fall down or bend over. One could see the families even in death. They were still holding hands."

Gerstein believed that if the German people were made aware of this horror, they would demand that the camps be shut down and the killing stopped. Jeopardizing his life, Gerstein told the pope's representative in Berlin what he had seen. He also wrote reports and passed them on to the Swedish embassy and to the Dutch Resistance. Gerstein's testimony and his letters were generally ignored. Many diplomats believed that Gerstein's stories were too horrible to be true.

The killing slowed down only when the Allies began to overrun the camps at the end of the war. The Holocaust ended with the final Allied victory in Europe.

When the victorious Allies seized the concentration camps, they found horrifying evidence of Nazi atrocities. At nearly every camp, hundreds of unburied bodies were lying about. These were found at Belsen (above) and Buchenwald (below).

Left: The Landsberg camp commandant stands amid some of his victims. Above: The women guards at Belsen were just as brutal as male guards in their treatment of inmates. Center left: Row after row of slain prisoners at Nordhausen. Below: About fifty open boxcars at Dachau were discovered to contain bodies. Bottom, both pictures: Stacks of bodies awaiting burial at Bergen-Belsen

These women dying of typhus and starvation were found at Belsen, where only a few days before, Anne Frank had died from the same causes.

The story of the Holocaust must focus on the millions of Jews who suffered and died during those nightmare years. One of them was Anne Frank, a young Jewish girl who spent most of the war years hiding with her family in an attic in Amsterdam. She was finally captured and eventually died of typhus in the Belsen concentration camp. Her diary, published in 1947, brings tears to the eyes of readers.

Under the Nazis, the Jews starved, bled, fought, and died, yet somehow kept their ancient culture intact. This song, sung by ghetto dwellers in Poland, captures the desperation felt by the Jewish people who lived through the Holocaust era:

Our brothers across the ocean
Cannot feel our bitter pain.
They cannot feel our bitter anguish
As death lurks over us every moment.
The war will end some day.
The world will realize the unheard-of horror.
Our Jewish heart is filled with pain:
Who will be able to heal our hurt?
Rivers of tears will flow
When they will find some day
The biggest grave in the world.

This bronze statue of a shrunken, skeletal inmate was unveiled
on the site of the Dachau crematorium on the fifth anniversary
of the entry of American troops who liberated the camp.

Index

About the Author

Mr. Stein was born and grew up in Chicago. At eighteen he enlisted in the Marine Corps where he served three years. He was a sergeant at discharge. He later received a B.A. in history from the University of Illinois and an M.F.A. from the University of Guanajuato in Mexico.

Although he served in the Marines, Mr. Stein believes that wars are a dreadful waste of human life. He agrees with a statement once uttered by Benjamin Franklin: "There never was a good war or a bad peace." But wars are all too much a part of human history. Mr. Stein hopes that some day there will be no more wars to write about.